MW01474714

All rights reserved. No part of this publication may be reproduced, distributed, or transmitted in any form or by any means, including photocopying, recording, or other electronic or mechanical methods, without the prior written permission of the publisher, except in the case of brief quotations embodied in critical reviews and certain other noncommercial uses permitted by copyright law.

Laughing Cat Publishing titles are also available at discount for retail, wholesale, promotional, and bulk purchase. For details, contact the Sales Manager by e-mail at youngwitchdeck@gmail.com

Written by Rebecca Jade

First printing edition 2020

ISBN: 978-0-9995665-5-8

Laughing Cat Publishing
Portland, Oregon.

Young Witch 101
A Beginner's Guide for Aspiring Witches

By Rebecca Jade

This book belongs to:

_____

Table of Contents

6-8	Introduction
9-10	Deciding Your "Path"
11-13	Meditation
14	Grimoires
15-18	Crystals
19-23	Herbs
24-30	Chakras
31-33	Elements
34	Familiars
35	Animal Signs
36-37	Bells
38-40	Wands
41-43	Candles

For Bedstefar, because different is not a bad thing, right? Mostly, for Eddie, Bel-Bel, Brodie, and Oliver; The most magical journey I have ever been on. Keep growing.

Introduction

Before I started school, my family moved to the rainforest of Victoria, Australia. A remote hideaway, dewy with fog that covered the forest and hugged the ancient tree ferns in its cold embrace.

My paternal grandmother would take me walking through the dense forest and down to the creek where we would sit on the creek bed staring at the messmate trees with their deep caverns at the base, waiting for the fae to come and join us. Sitting quietly, we would breathe gently and not say a word, listening to the sounds of the forest. And then I would get goosebumps, my hair would stand on end, and for a moment everything would go perfectly still and quiet. It was then my grandmother would whisper to me, "They're here. I know you feel it, too." It was in these times I knew I was "different."

But how to understand this—that was another challenge. My friends didn't have the answers; they all thought I was a bit weird, and maybe they were right. I didn't have the nicest clothes or the best manners, but I had a lot of ideas, that's for sure.

So I went to my parents and I asked them what they knew about "different." I found out that "different" meant "gifted" and "interesting" in my family; and so my father allowed me to peruse all of his books on witching, from ancient work to root work to ritual and self-discovery through meditation and yoga.

So many Young Witches don't have access to this, or they do not have a community to help them find the answers to light the lantern to their path of spiritual work. That's why I wrote this booklet. Because all Young Witches have to start somewhere, right?

Here I have collated years of collected information from people I love that I have stored in my very own grimoire. I have sifted through to make it relevant to a wide audience that can use it in practical and effective ways to build upon their own desire to uplift themselves and those around them. I have incorporated information from many religious backgrounds, as there is much for Young Witches to learn from all faiths, with the aim of it being readable, accessible, and affordable.

While this is certainly not a full list of what can be achieved, it is a basic kit for a beginner. You may think you'll never need some of the information within, such as chakra correspondence. Let me tell you that all correspondence is good and all of the magical realms are indeed linked. There is more to learn after this, so please research, look, find, observe. Be safe.

As an elder, I can tell you now that if I had a book like this when I was younger, I would certainly be further along in my practice now than I currently am. I am a solitary Eclectic Witch, and I love where this witching journey has taken me. I have read tarot since I was a young teenager, and I practice my craft every day of my life.

I hope that this book finds you standing in your power and ready to learn, Young Witch. May your future be bright and prosperous with the aid of the knowledge held within this cover.

Deciding Your "Path"

A "Path" refers to the kind of Young Witch you want to be, kind of like a denomination. Are you a Wiccan or a Kitchen Witch? A Garden Witch? Eclectic? SO MANY WORDS, OH MY GODS! Wait. Don't even get me started on the gods. We're just going to cut all the rubbish out of this and get down to it.

Choosing things that suit you and your personal choice and power is called "Eclectic." This might not suit everyone. A Witch who practices her craft solo and doesn't need others to perform spells, or only gets help from her witchy friends sometimes, is called a "Solitary Witch." Anyone who follows strict rules, the rule of three (that which you do will come back to you threefold) may be a Wiccan.

Your path is entirely your choice, and it may change over time. You will learn from others, and you will learn from yourself; your path and practice will grow and change as you do—it is about you, after all.

Young Witch, please remember that what others see as right or wrong, light or dark, is not for you to take on board. You must follow your calling and trust that you are doing what is right for you in any given time. Seek guidance from your elders if you are in doubt, and gather wise crones who will assist you. There are many Mother Witches and crones out there who love to see Young Witches bloom and blossom, yet be sure to always remember this:

If you lead yourself with trust, respect, and honesty, you will never fail yourself, and your path, whatever that may be, will always be well lit.

Travel well. Travel lightly. Travel safely. Travel freely.

Meditation for Young Witches

You might think that meditating is all "Ommmmmms" and making your mind empty while crossing your legs like some kind of pretzel—mmmm pretzels. We haven't even started yet and it's already easy to get distracted—oooft! Forget about all of that. All you have to do is follow these simple instructions:

- **Get comfy**. Just don't lie down because you might go to sleep! Sit on your bed, on the floor, in a chair . . . it doesn't really matter.

- **Set your intention**. Whaaaaaaaat? I know. It sounds ridiculous! But by deciding what you want to achieve in your meditation before you meditate, you'll get a better result. So, if I've had a bad day and want to relax, I'll say out loud "I wish to be peaceful" before I begin.

- **Grab your quartz points**! As you will see in your basic crystal guide, quartz amplifies all energies and helps the person holding it to obtain a clear mind and a clear purpose.

- **Forget about all that drivel about clearing your mind**. You will think. A lot. And that's OK;, in fact, it's really, really important! Hear the thoughts, acknowledge them, and go on to the next step—focusing on your breath.

- **Breathe**. This is it, Witches. What it's all about. Some people call it "breathing for peace," but this is how it's done. Breathe into your diaphragm. That's breathing so your stomach pushes out and in, not your chest. Slowly breathe in for the count of seven, hold for the count of three, release the breath to the count of ten, hold for three, and start all over again.

It seems really hard at first, and it can be; that's true. But once you get the hang of it, you will be flying through the astral plane like you've always been there.

Dos and Don'ts

- Don't keep trying to count if you run out of breath—ever! If you feel short of breath, just breathe normally, and get your caregivers or a friend to check on you.

- Don't think it has to be perfect. Perfect is what suits you. This is your craft, your practice, and your spiritual journey. Don't ever forget that.

- Do keep trying. Even if you're just standing in the shower or waiting in line for the bus. Some of the best breath work I have done has been with my eyes open in random places; practice, practice, practice!

- Do write/record/acknowledge your experiences as you start meditating. It's good to look back at them and see how far you've come.

Huh? Grimiore?

Sounds awful, right? Grim, gross and ugly . . . well, I suppose sometimes they can be. They can be messy, have things spilled on them, and pages that are torn and ruffled beyond measure. "Uhhh.. that's great Becca . . . but what is it?"

Well it's not a jar of eyeballs, or newts, or chicken feet. It's a spell book, a witches guide to all the things they have learned and they are lifelong. You never stop writing and many witches have volumes of them. You may have also heard it "referred to as a Book of Shadows." You can call it whatever you like; call it Herbert. (Hey, that's a great name for a plant guide!) Or Rhonda . . . I dunno, whatever you call it, keep what you learn in it and never stop; even if you think that the information is useless, like something you tried and it didn't work. Why? Because you will know how to change it in the future.

Beginner's crystals

Clear Quartz – Amplifies any energy around it, including your energy, your tools, and even your other crystals. While it helps you to find patience to cleanse your heart and mind, it is also an excellent all-rounder. Clear quartz can be carried with you everywhere, kept by your bed, and used during your meditations. Each piece of this "master healer" was hand chosen for your Young Witch bag.

Rose Quartz – Teaches you to grab your natural gifts in the arts, to use your own love to help the world, and most of all, to love yourself as you truly are. Rose quartz will help you to be more grounded and loving in all things and to let go of feeling like you need to compete for attention, because the person who needs your adoration the most is sometimes you.

Amethyst– Brings you peace, calm, and tranquillity. Amethyst will also boost your dreams and insights in your daily life. Keeping some by your bed and near your witching tools will help increase your dream power, too! It is also a protection crystal, so be sure to have some around to keep any nasty energy out of your field, Young Witch!

Selenite – Keep it clean with selenite! You can put your other crystals near selenite to cleanse them in between moon cycles, and you can keep it around to keep your space feeling clear and free of negative attachments, too. Selenite is also great for keeping things calm; being a Young Witch is often full of highs and lows, so it's helpful to have around.

Lapis Lazuli – The stone you want around to increase your psychic powers and protect you from anyone throwing psychic shade your way, Lapis Lazuli has been sought after for thousands of years; if it was good enough for young King Tut to have adorning his royal jewels and burial garb, it's good enough for us! Lapis Lazuli helps you to accept your path in this life and be the best you can be. It's great for your memory and study, too.

Pyrite – Otherwise known as "Fool's Gold," but anyone would be foolish to mess around with the person who uses pyrite in their magic and meditations! Pyrite boosts self-esteem and self-worth, draws in prosperity (cash dollllahhs, Witches!) protects you from harm, helps you stand your ground . . . Look, Young Witch. Trust me. Pyrite is often so overlooked as a starter stone because it's cheap and accessible, but it's soSO powerful that it's like a spiritual UFO invasion.

Black Obsidian – Absorbs all negativity and cleanses any bad vibes. Need I say more?

Green Fluorite – Healing is beautiful, Young Witch! Green fluorite is great for healing communication problems and sore hearts. Let's face it; it's better to heal your heart from a nasty break up than try to turn the ex into your next familiar. It won't end well, or so I've heard *looks around suspiciously*. In all seriousness, green fluorite is also a great stone to keep close for anyone wanting to lift their brain power, too; a smart Witch is a good Witch.

Labradorite – Labradorite is a grounder of spiritual energy, so it helps you to draw down your natural magical abilities and use them strongly and wisely, while keeping you balanced and protected in your practice. Not only that, it's awesome for Young Witches in particular, helping you show the world your maturity and fun side at the same time. So grab some labradorite, wear it and use it with pride, and show the world who you are with a smile on your face—because we are soooo ready for you, Witches!

Buuut why didn't they say anything about **citrine**, huh? Good question. Because that gross, hard looking orange and deep, dark yellow stuff (wait for it) isn't actually citrine at all! It's baked amethyst. They cook the amethyst in a hot oven and the purple turns an orange or yellow color and they sell it as citrine—what a rip off! Real citrine is gorgeous, mottled with clear quartz and the most brilliant and bright yellows. It is also RIDIC on the price scale. If you can find it, afford it, and you vibe with it, by all means purchase it.

But the starters provided are well enough to get any Young Witch moving along nicely. They are also available in price ranges that are affordable across the world so that you can use pocket money, job money, or you can pool gift money to buy them for your witchy friends for their birthdays, too.

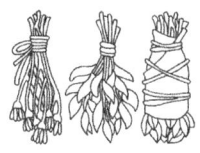

Beginner's Plants and Herbs

There are many plants and herbs used in witching, so many that you'd need a whole book just to get you started, and then you'd need a college degree to understand the whole thing anyway . . . but you don't need all of that. So many plants can be foraged or may even be in your garden right now! But you don't have a garden , you say? You live in an apartment in the city? Check around your local park or botanical garden and see if your local hardware store has these to start a little window garden if you're able!

Wormwood – This gorgeous plant comes in green or silver. She has a variety of uses including reversing spells, hex removal, love spells, cleansing, and smudging, not to mention its use in divination and scrying. Wormwood can be crushed and burned. Be careful burning wormwood, as it can irritate your throat. Use only under the supervision and strict guidance of an elder.

Lavender – A great calming herb, lavender is also useful in banishing harmful spirits and calming any negative energies in your field. Use it in reversals and magic to boost your school scores, too! Be careful with lavender, as it is one of those herbs people can be ultra-allergic to. But if you're not allergic, cut a few stems and pop them in your pillowcase to help you sleep at night, add a few stems to a warm bath, or put them in the bottom of the shower to release the oils for a nice calming effect.

Rue (or Ruda) – Oddly enough cats don't like it, so keep it away from your feline familiar! It has also been used to keep away bad Witches since the dawn of magic, so DO use it in all evil eye reversals and hex returns. Rue is a great protector and will keep you safe. You can bunch it up and rub it or gently tap it on yourself to cleanse yourself, you can add it to a cleansing bath, and if you wanna get ultra-witchy with it, rue is always used on witchy holidays, as it is fantastic for money, love, and (in case I haven't said it enough) protection spells! RUE!

Mint – Tie a bunch of it near your front door and bring in some good vibes and good friends. Mint can help to get the conversation flowing, make your relationships sweeter (including the ones between you and your parents and teachers!), and it can also help you to get over some of your fears, so kick your phobias and social anxieties in the pants with mint!

Basil – Get yourself some happy, some money, some protection, some cleansing and calm with basil! You can eat it, hang it up, and even chew it after you've eaten to expel those, ermmm, toot tooters. I mean, the dog's ones. Yeah, those. *cough* Don't eat heaps though, because bulk amounts aren't great for Young Witches or pregnant people and all herbs should be taken with supervision from your elders and medical professionals OK? OK!

Salt – YOU NEED THIS! Sea salt all the way, Young Witch! You've probably seen all the Witches in movies make salt circles to protect themselves or make big-time magic; it's a real thing! You put a line of salt across your doorways and window frames to protect you from negative energies and spells, and you can sprinkle salt around the house and vacuum it up after a few hours to absorb the negative energy in the house. You can add epsom salts to a bath to cleanse yourself (absolutely make a potion with any of the other herbs that you can bathe with to make it a beautiful ritual for yourself— just don't forget to make sure you're not allergic to anything first and that you've got help from an elder on hand.).

Black salt is like super powered Witch salt that will remove all negativity and send it right back with a punch. If you are using black salt, please follow the directions carefully and if it is magical salt DO NOT EAT IT, OK? EVER!

Pure Incense – This is a resin incense that churches use ("WHAAAT? CHURCH?!?!" I hear you ask). Bear with me. Even though Witches and churches have a horrible history, we really aren't too far apart. There is much magic that happens in those places, and they use some pretty cool stuff that we Witches use, so stick with me for a second.

Pure incense is often confused as plain old frankincense, yet it is much more complex. It contains many ingredients that are holy to churches and Young Witches, too— frankincense, myrrh, benzoin, copal, styrax, sandalwood, and cedar. All of these resins are burned for purification on charcoal disks in a censer (metal incense burner), the same as any Witch would do, how funny hey?

You can buy incense from orthodox church shops that are open often (usually at the front) and these are great places to buy beeswax candles really cheaply, too!

If you don't want to go to a church, that's cool, there's a lot of history there to unpack. You can buy it online or head to your local Greek, Aegean, or Slavic deli. They will stock it as well as rose incense, charcoal disks, and candles. They will also have a lot of the herbs listed in this book, but keep an eye out for anti-evil eye talismans and various good luck charms. A lot of witching practice came from these places and they have the goods so a lot of our stuff crosses over.

Don't be afraid to explore, Young Witch. History can be scary, but it can be really enlightening, too.

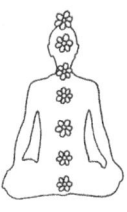

Chakras

Not the things that go on your feet, or those little clacky hand instruments — they're canastas and you can dance with them later. Say it together — CHUCK-RAHHHH.

Originating in Hinduism, chakra means "wheel" in Sanskrit and can be found in Vedic scripts dating back to around 500 BC. That's as old as some of our witching practice, so it for sure belongs here. So, to put it simply, each chakra is a different color because each one represents a different energy centre in the body.

The first chakra – Root Chakra; Sanskrit: Muladhara. Color: Red; Sound: LAM

Situated at the base of the spine, just below your hips, the root chakra is connected to your primal self and drives. These are your needs to sleep, eat, protect your ego, and uhhh, reproduce? (Awkward.) If the root chakra is blocked, you might have some fears or get nightmares a lot! Wear more red—put some red undies on and rock your day! Meditate on your sound, and hang on to that clear quartz, too.

The second chakra – Sacral Chakra; Sanskrit: Svadhisthana. Color: Orange; Sound: VAM

Situated in the middle of the pelvis, the sacral chakra is connected to your creative self, emotions, sexual energy (not just procreation, but wanting to chase after a partner), and your shadow self. So, this energy centre is there to regulate our primal self and to not be owned by it. When it is humming along like a well-oiled machine, you will feel like making friends, having a good time, and like you've got it pretty good on this mortal coil overall. But if it's blocked, you're going to have a bad time. You'll be feeling stuck, have creative blocks all over the shop, you won't be able to think or write or draw or act or sing or anything you like doing creatively that I can't even think of right now (Wait! Is my sacral blocked!?), and you might get bouts of sadness or feeling like you want to eat the whole pantry without any medical reason. Do wear orange, do chant your sound in meditation, do use your labradorite and clear quartz to help move things along.

The third chakra – Solar Plexus Chakra; Sanskrit: Manipura; Color: Yellow; Sound: RAM

Situated around your belly button, the solar plexus chakra is your drive and determination! When it is in alignment, the third chakra will help you to know what serves you and what needs the chop—it's all about that gut feeling, right? When it is blocked, you may feel unable to trust yourself and your decisions or instincts, or worse, feel badly about yourself. You are beautiful and amazing, Young Witch! Tell yourself in the mirror, practice meditating on the color yellow, and repeat the sound for the chakra as you meditate. It's a great idea to lie around with your pyrite on your tummy, too!

The fourth chakra – Heart Chakra; Sanskrit: Anahata. Color: Green; Sound: YAM

Situated in the middle of your chest, the heart chakra will show you unconditional love for yourself, how to love people even if they cannot be in your life, and how to let go of toxic people and situations with a peaceful energy. It's the real vibe of "That person is an absolute doorknob, but the right thing to do is *insert correct and lawful action here* and so that's what I'm going to do." Someone with a blocked heart space is going to be stuck in feeling like they can't stand up for themselves, or they have to stay in toxic situations, or worse, like they cannot speak up about bad things that have happened to them. You can, and you should, live your best and most authentic life where it is safe and possible. Wear some more green, put that fluorite over your heart space and meditate on it. Witches everywhere believe in you and your future, Young Witch.

The fifth chakra- Throat Chakra; Sanskrit: Vishuddha. Color: Blue, Sound: HAM

Situated at the base of the neck, the throat chakra is all about living and speaking your most authentic and honest self. If it's blocked, you won't be able to tell people how you really feel, and you will struggle to hold space for yourself. You might even worry about being judged by people around you or struggle to stay focused, so lie down with some lapis lazuli on your neck and meditate on it. Chant your chakra sound and sing! Open up your voice and go to a hill and scream from a mountain if you can. If all you have is sign language or a communication board or pictures, bust out those swears and tell the universe how you really feel, Young Witch! Stretch your neck by moving it from side to side and open it up. Let's get this voice!

The sixth chakra – Third Eye Chakra; Sanskrit: Ajna, Color: Indigo; Sound: OM

Situated between your eyebrows, the third eye is all about your intuition, not the gut feeling, but the real inner knowing, your psychic self. It also rules over how you interact with the world around you, how you move through the world and carve your path in it, Young Witch. If it's blocked you might act like a bit of an all-round, world class jerk actually. You'll probably be judgmental of others, not want to listen to others' world views, and sadly, this might interfere with how you learn things, too. It's cool though, we can change it! Put some amethyst on your third eye and chant your sound. Work your other chakras, too, because if your third eye is struggling, you likely have a block somewhere else too.

The seventh chakra – Crown Chakra; Sanskrit: Sahasrara; Color: White/Violet; Sound: OM

This one is at the top of your head. Just as the name suggests, it's right where a crown would sit. It lets you get downloads from the universe and know that you're a part of something much bigger than one person, bigger than eight billion people, but so small that it could fit in your hand all at once and all you'll ever need to know is love and that love isn't hearts, chocolates, stuffed bears, and flowers; love is honesty, self-discovery, space, and growth—even when it's painful.

When it's blocked, you will feel alone even when you have a big support group around you, and you won't feel connected to your space and your own power. Unblocking your crown is not as easy as the other chakras, this comes with time and effort, you must work at it every day and know that you are working towards your enlightenment.

Practice as you would any other chakra; hold your rose quartz, chant your sound, and meditate. Practice love with yourself and forgiving yourself for mistakes and recognizing your growth. Be patient with yourself and others./ Please understand that you are not perfect, but neither is anyone else. What you are is learning, changing, growing, and moving. That is beautiful.

I really like your Hara…

We talk a lot about your spirit, but what is it? Well, in the ancient Japanese Zen Shiatsu (not Shitzu) theory, it is your Hara, the centre of the body. If you think of a clock face that sits in your stomach and connects to all of your vital organs, creating a roadmap to the rest of your body, it is your own centre, the engine, where all good things are made—the place of Ki, or energy. You have to take care of your own Hara

before you can take care of someone else's, because you cannot help someone fill up if you are empty, too. So please, Young Witch, do look out for your community, do look out for your friends and family, but always, make sure that you take care of your Hara, because so much of your work comes from there.
Chakra- Solar Plexus.

Elements

Earth****Air****Fire****Water****Spirit

These are the basic elements incorporated into any magical working.

Things that are Earthly are dirt, rocks, sticks, plants, and the like. A little bit of salt on your magical space is a good Earth addition. Metal is also Earth elemental and anything that comes from the Earth will ground your energy; this in part is why you have beautiful sleigh bells for cleansing—but more on those later! The great thing about metal is that you can even just use music! Heavy metal music of any kind is elemental, too! Turn it up loud (maybe we should have put some earplugs in these bags, ha ha!) and let the Earth element change your energy and increase your magic.

Things that are of Air include smoke from incense or smudging, feathers used to fan, and dancing is Air elemental too! If it's too cold to open a window or you can't burn incense, shake whatcha Mama gave ya! Don't forget to check in with an elder when burning incense or smudging, because fires happen easily, and we want you safe! If you can't use smoke to cleanse, rely on an Earthly and grounding cleansing with your bells! Always open your windows and doors to let the Air circulate for a truer elemental cleansing.

Things that are Fiery include bonfires,, candles, the sun! Stand in the sunshine (with the proper protection of course). Young Witches, you must remember that *all* forms of Fire energy are wild and can cause you harm if you're not careful, so check in with an elder when working with Fire! If you can't use flame for this element, you can add red and orange or gold colors to your space.

Things that are of Water include natural bodies of Water like lakes, streams, rivers, oceans, rain, and even baths, showers, the Water you drink, and cups of delicious tea. But if you don't have any Water hanging around, you can use the sound of it, too! If you are sad, your tears are Water as well. Don't forget that you can make Moon Water, Storm Water, and all kinds of powerful magical Waters that will boost your magic by taking a jar, filling it with drinkable Water, putting a cap on it and putting it out in the weather/moon event you want to utilize.

Need to cleanse some tools? Storm Water. Need to tell someone off? Lightning! Need to add some power? Full moon! Need to get all heavy and mystical with it? Dark moon. Awwwww yeah!

Things that are of Spirit, well, that's you, Young Witch. You are the Spirit element in everything. You are the centre of your work at all times. You are looking out for yourself, putting yourself at the centre, and invoking the Spirit of all Witches who have come before you as you step into your own power and make your own kind of magic. You are the One. The God Particle, the Essence, the Missing Link, the je ne sais quoi; you are the Universe in motion. We all are, and you are calling on all of us when you work, even if you are solitary. TEAM WITCH!

Familiars

Like family?

Yeah, kind of! But with fur, feathers, scales, and claws! Pets are our spiritual counterparts, and they imprint on us. They protect our energy and help us do work through our connection to them. Do we need them? Absolutely not. Not every Witch has a familiar, just like not every Witch uses crystals or herbs. But if a familiar is a part of your path, it's OK if it's not a cat; all kinds of pets can be familiars to a Young Witch, you just need a psychic connection to them, a special bond that only you two have.

Animal Signs

Have you ever had a crow calling outside your window that big, loud, "HAW HAW!" only to get news later in the day that you didn't get the marks you wanted on that miserable math test? Yep, your crow friend was trying to prepare you. Have you had a blue colored bird bop in front of you tirelessly when you're feeling down? It's reminding you that it's time to have some fun and live in the moment, Young Witch!

As you continue on your path, you will notice nature connecting with you in strange ways and animals popping up to say hello in many forms. Look for the signs, look them up. Give thanks for the message you received and if you feel so driven, keep a journal of the signs that nature gives you, it will help you recognize them in the future.

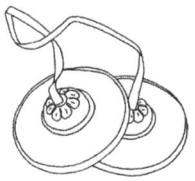

Bells, the Bells!

In your hand-picked, hand-packed Young Witch bag you will find three cute little brass clearing bells. These bells are made in Tibet, and are for space clearing. Metal is excellent for clearing spaces of any kind of stagnant energy, it vibrates when you hit it, and this makes bells the perfect tool for any Young Witch.

How to use them:

Hold the bells by the ribbon and practice your meditation breathing. Gently shake the bells around the thing you want to cleanse. You can cleanse your Young Witch Deck, your room, your familiar, your best friend, and, if you're feeling really brave, maybe your folks! They are especially good for your altar and any tools you are using like candles or ribbons as well.
At Young Witch, we like to keep our bells pinned to us in the tradition of sleigh bells. In times of heavy snow, the gentle jingle would be sent off through the white mist, protecting the driver

from bad spirits, keeping the traveling path clear by alerting them to the obstacles, but also sending the sound waves back to protect others walking alone in the forest, because those who cannot see the danger need our help the most.

In all magical folklore, we Witches have gotten a bad rap. I mean, whole pieces of history have sought to have us removed, but we have stayed and practiced our arts and wishes in private and groups or covens for millennia. Here's where that image of the Witch hiding in the woods, slaving over a hot cauldron and covering her house in candy comes in (what do we want, ants? No. A house covered in candy is exactly how you get ants. Haven't they ever heard of pizza?)

Slavic legend Baba Yaga could be the highlight of all of these. Mortar and pestle driving, man eating, chicken house living, mad woman they say . . . but what do they leave out? That she will honor you if you have a good heart and intent, and that is what this craft, this practice, this path is all about—your intent. You can look scary, you can have a bad reputation, you can have wild hair, and yet, just like Baba Yaga, you can command the sun, moon, and stars. But at the end of it all, people will know you by your heart.

Wands

Some Young Witches might like to use a wand. A good wand needs only a few key ingredients, and it needs to suit you.

To make a wand from natural wood, there are many options to choose from! I highly recommend researching what wood you would most like to use, as you can have many wands for many different occasions, but for the best all round and most magical use, oak is the way to go.

To select your oak branch, go with your caregiver to a tree that you know you can get a branch from legally and safely and select one that will fit nicely in your hand. You will harvest it, always asking the tree for permission. (Would you like it if someone cut off one of your branches without asking first? Probably not.)

Let it dry out somewhere warm for about a month until it's a dry stick, then oil it, and prepare it how you wish. You can carve them (with assistance) and add embellishments such as crystals, found feathers, and other items of your choice. To bless your wand for use you just need:

Salt water
A candle
A lit stick of incense

Gather all of your tools and your wand in front of you, and here's what you can do:

Sprinkle the wand with the salt water for the elements of Earth (North) and Water (West).

Pass the wand quickly, so it doesn't catch fire, through the candle flame for the element of Fire (South,)

and then gently pass it through the incense smoke for the element of Air (East).

Last, hold the wand close to your heart for the element of Spirit (Centre) and repeat, "I bless this wand from the centre of me, to be used for only the highest good, so mote it be."

Repeat your blessing as often as you need. If this blessing is not your style, feel free to write your own.

You don't have to take a branch either. You can use a sturdy fallen branch, a nice piece of driftwood, anything lovely wand-shaped that catches your eye.

Really, you can even bless a kitchen whisk or a chisel if you really want! My favorite wands are letter openers. Why? Because they deliver messages, that's what they were made for. So, eyes peeled, Young Witch, you'll be surprised at what catches you.

Candle Magic

You probably hear a lot about Witches using candles for things, and when you see them in the movies the "good" Witches are burning white candles and the "bad" ones have black candles. Well! Let's blow all of that right out of the water because candles are great spells and healers and should be on every Young Witches radar with a little help from their caregiver. First, what kind?

Chime candles are small, thin, and burn quickly. They're great if you want to get a spell or intention complete in a short time.

Taper candles you've probably seen on a dinner table. A regular taper candle burns for around six to eight hours if it's undressed (pyjamas not included).

Pillar candles, as the name suggests, look like the pillars out the front of old buildings. Sometimes called church or votive candles, they are thick and can come in glass cases or without. These are often used for seven-day or longer rituals.

What color?

White - All colors. You name it, white will do it.

Black - Absorbs negative energies; excellent for uncrossing and unblocking.

Red - Passion or anger, use when you're wanting to add a little spice to the spell.

Pink - Emotional work such as love, family, friendship.

Purple - All things divine and magical. Enhance spell work, get closer to your guardians.

Blue - Protection, peace, anything to do with education and work.

Yellow - Intellect, clear thought, and for a boost to money spells.

Green - Growth, healing, and fertility; especially in finances.

Silver - For manifestation and connection to lunar energy.

Gold - Success, luck, and attraction. Solar energy.

So, I was kidding about the pyjamas. When you dress a candle, you use oils and herbs with the help of your caregiver. You apply the dressing that matches what you want to achieve.

For instance, if you were having trouble with a bunch of bullies at school, you would take a black candle and write your name on it with a stick or a pen or anything that would leave a mark. Then you would rub a little lavender oil on it and sprinkle some rue from the herbs list. You would then watch the candle to make sure it didn't burn anything, until it burnt out. You would repeat the spell three times, letting the negative bully energy be returned back to the universe in a calm state, hopefully leaving you alone. A peaceful solution for all.

OK, So What Now?

Now you know some basic, and not-so-basic, information about witching, what it means to be a Young Witch, how to take care of your energy, and basic tools. It's all up to you.

We can't tell you how to follow your path or choose your adventure, Young Witch, but we really do hope that you will take the knowledge in this booklet that has been collected from my own grimoire from years of education from my elders and word of mouth from my circle, and you will forge your own path. Read, write, research, and throw yourself into what it means to be you.

Because your education, of any kind, is the best investment you will ever make, as it will ultimately lead to your growth.

Made in the USA
Monee, IL
13 December 2023